hongdandan

tonight

only

one

hongdandan

blue day

hongdandan

hongdandan

tulip

hongdandan

the way to meet 1

the way to meet 2

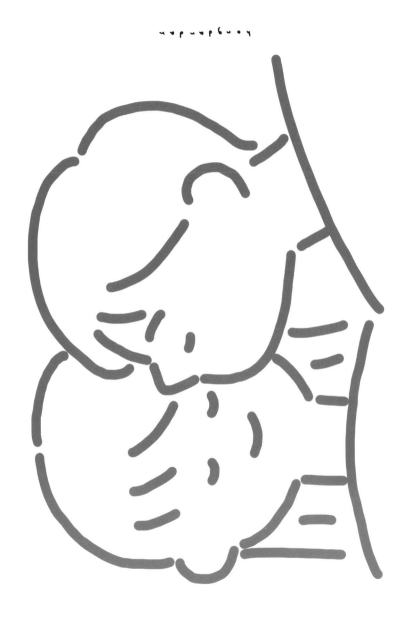

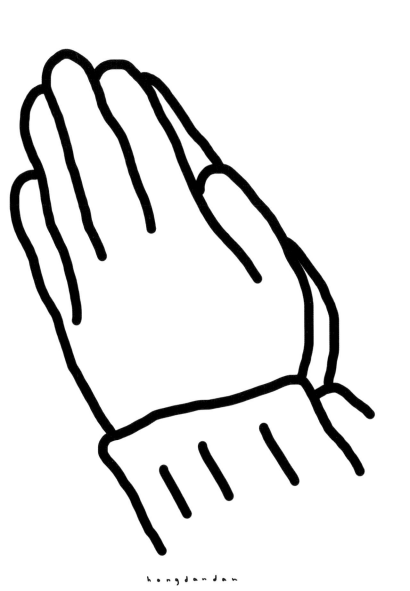

hongdandan

pray without ceasing

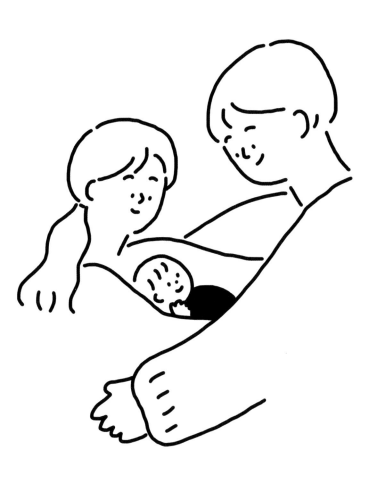

hongdandan

hongdandan

meal

acorn

hongdandan

my sweety

hongdandan

flower

hongdandan

waiting for you

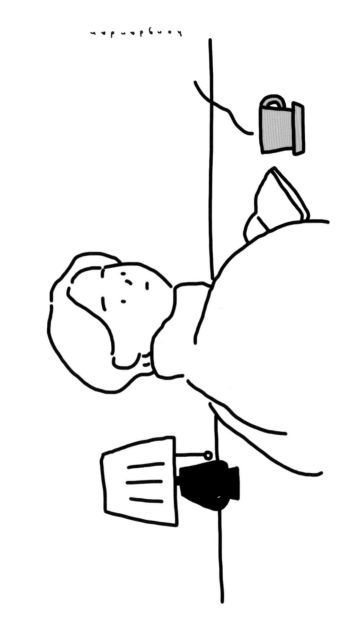

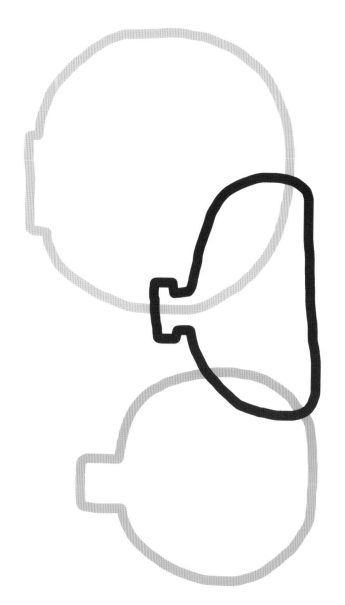

object

sweet heart

hongdandan

love you

breakfast

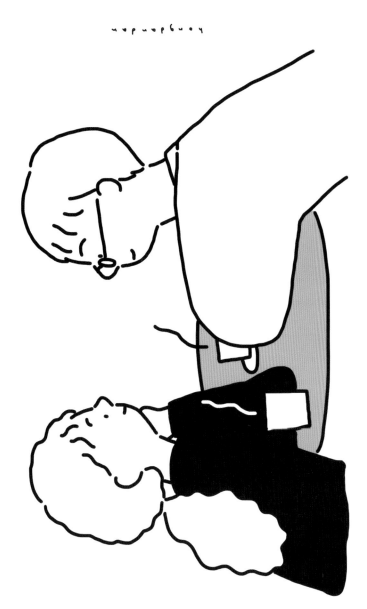

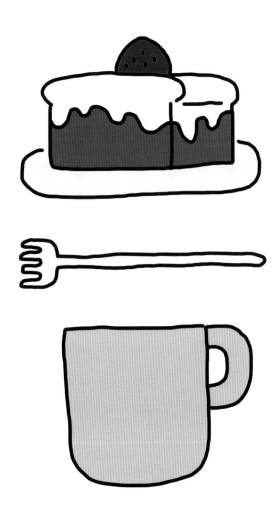

coffee

POST

missed you

missed you too

BIG LOVE

hongdandan

comfy

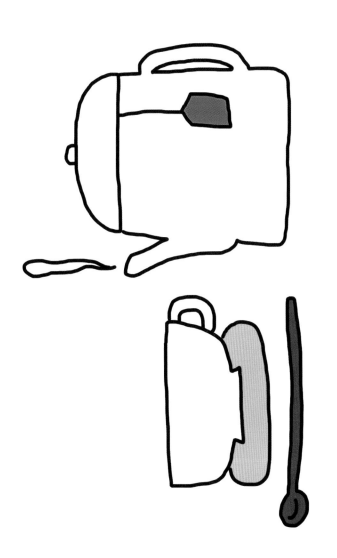

flower 2

hongdandan

friend

hongdandan

hello

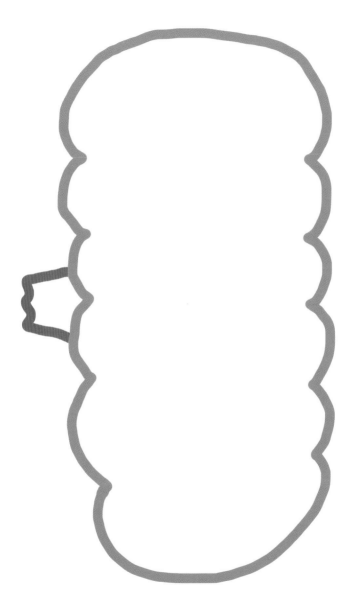

*forest*

hongdandan

hug

hongdandan

tonight

hongdandan

cat

hongdandan

the way to meet

'

the way to meet 2

hongdandan

acorn

hongdandan

waiting for you

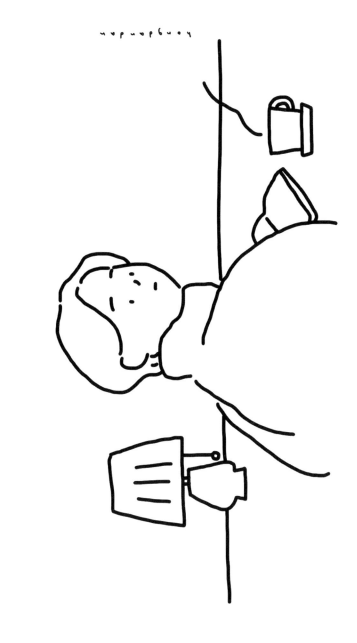

sweet heart

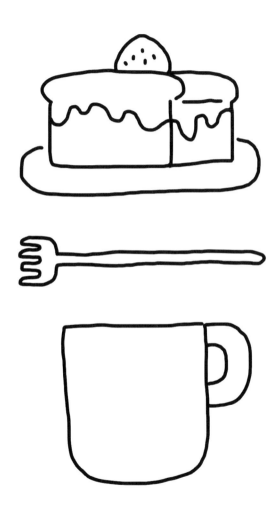

hongdandan

coffee

hongdandan

hug